A Look at My Love

Written by: Dillon Longtin

One thing you should know about me is,

I am really fond of history,

Sometimes more than that of my love for English,

A history that is most fond to me is,

Well,

Ours!

A Look At My Love

Ending a Chapter in life is scary, Especially when you have to go into the real

world.

One of my chapters was ending. My High School one,

And a new one was beginning.

My Life as an adult and the Infamous Navy.

I first found out I got orders to a country called Bahrain, I had no clue what this

place was where it was or what I was getting myself into, I was in bootcamp, It

almost felt unreal, when I was told you know, I couldn't believe it, I always

thought someway that my instructors where messing with me somehow and it was

all fake. The truth is I wanted to go home, that's where I was comfortable,

CALIFORNIA.

I suppressed it until I had to face it.

*

A Look At My Love

*

After I successfully made it through bootcamp and school it was the end of

September, and it was time for me to go home.

*

*

*

After a somewhat amazing leave I had to hop on a plane from San Francisco

International and be alone for the first time,

In order to start my real life.

Stepping off the plane in Norfolk was different,

I felt lonely, I was a lone wolf with no pack and nobody to guide me.

I was free roaming as a lone wolf would be,

I still remember walking through that long baggage claim hallway at 2 AM Alone

with nobody else in sight.

Here I would be informed that the AMC terminal was closed.

And no flights where coming or going.

In a way I felt relief, I wasn't ready to leave the states,

And I sure as hell wasn't expecting to find love.

A Look At My Love

Driving alone on a highway with barely another car in sight seeing

Virginia lights for the first time. I checked into TPU..

I remember it being really cold in the lobby,

I was freezing as the CDO took his time

issued a rack and an uncomfortable pillow

Feeling alone as ever and as cold as ever,

I didn't know what to do with myself.

But I found unhealthy ways to occupy myself.

I remember first seeing a picture of you,

I knew there was something there, something great,

I was in my rack looking out the window staring wondering where you could be, as

the leaves fell to the ground outside in the distance

I couldn't help but wonder had I just fallen for you too, maybe I was obsessed, I

had to get to know you.

It was a feeling.

I was drawn to you

As a dog is drawn to a bone or as a bee to a flower

I knew I needed you, I just didn't know why.

A Look At My Love

Our First date was magical,

I was so nervous I could barely eat.

I was about as nervous as a bird flying for the first time,

But somehow it all felt really natural

After that dinner,

WE had our first kiss In the parking lot outside your car.

I'd be lying if I said that that kiss didn't send me soaring.

I was flying I wasn't a baby bird anymore,

I was grown and I was soaring

That kiss had me flying,

I saw everything I needed to in that kiss.

It's almost as if I wasn't in my body

I was on the outside, Looking down upon us from heaven,

Our first kiss sent me to the angels,

And from then on I was obsessed.

OR I was in LOVE

A Look At My Love

Being with you I Forgot about everything. Leaving,

Being afraid,

I don't think you know this but I drew my strength to leave from you,

I had courage to leave because of you,

You sent me where I needed to be and you made me as strong as I needed to be.

As I left

Looking into your eyes

I feel okay

They are my most favorite feature about you

Your eyes.

They glisten

And they shine

they shined for me

Like the sun shines for the earth.

The Moments before the Moments that lead to this one, where

A Look At My Love

Perhaps the greatest of my life.

Being with you I felt Okay

I felt Secure, I felt loved.

Unfortunately

My cowerdess gave all that away when I left,

A piece of me stayed behind with you.

And I knew that which is why we tried to stay in touch.

*

In our middle ground,

Seeing you happy with other men made me sick.

My heart always belong to you even when we were not together,

I was fucked lashing out and ultimately broken.

Nobody made me happy unless I was truly talking to you.

I'm not sure why I kept pushing you away except I was afraid of something real

with you.

When I'm not with you I made terrible decisions.

My headspace was worse than ever before.

I think I had to let you go because I don't think my heart fully loved you yet. I

needed to get to know you more,

I'm not sure why I thought I could do that a part away from each other.

A Look At My Love

*

*

*

I knew to myself on my way back to the states for Christmas that it wouldn't feel

real until I actually could see you.

*

Suddenly I was having flashbacks, When I landed in Norfolk,

For the second time,

Everything was coming back to me.

Walking down a long baggage claim area in a cold airport.

Recanting every memory I had in that airport.

I think it was easier for me to suppress our memories together,

It made it easier for me to try not to love you.

Being in Norfolk with you Jogged my memory,

By the end of my time with you I Remembered everything,

Down to the last detail.

Driving down certain streets made me remember things that I have suppressed for

a year.

A Look At My Love

It was painful to remember, but I needed to in order to remember

How much I love you.

*

*

One day driving alone in your car I suddenly get a feeling of déjà vu

I've been here before,

I've done this before.

That's what it felt like my entire time with you.

And my future life with you.

*

Being with you again was like reliving my past life,

Being with a past love of mine.

I believe that we all have past lives,

I also believe you have been the love of my life for all of them.

Tyler, I don't know if you can feel it or not.

But our souls are connected.

Our souls met in the heavens and when they came down to earth they were

destined to meet each other again, and again.

You are my great love the one I'm destined to be with forever.

I can honestly say that without you I am not myself.

A Look At My Love

_____

I didn't know I was lost going through this life aimlessly until I found you. Tyler I

don't know what I would have been or done without you.

*

Now I can't imagine not being tied with you.

*

My heart cannot take this distance, being away from you creates an unimaginable

pain. However I am suffering through it for you.

I know one day our stars will realign. I know that we will always move a

mountain for each other. I know that no matter what we will find some way

somehow to make this work and make us work.

My ultimate goal is with you my ultimate family is with you.

You are the only thing I want in this world more than anything.

Nothing else matters when I'm with you,

So I am sorry if I am really protective of us and how fragile our love is.

I believe in soulmates, and soulmates are supposed to be easy.

I believe in you and I believe in us more than anything I have ever believed in this

world. My full faith is riding in us.

A Look At My Love

Today was a hard day… And today you proved to me that no matter what you will always be there for me. I know sometimes I can implode like a bonfire on a Saturday night with the boys in the country and the heat can be almost unbearable but you didn't go anywhere you stayed and stuck by me. Today you validated me and made me feel better. The way you already know how to handle me exposes that you already know so much about me you know how to calm me down. You know how to treat me. You know how to cool down the fire when its boring too bright in the pale moonlight. Today you made me realize that you will drop whatever you are doing in order to make me feel like me again. You proved yourself to me and your loyalty. I feel better, for now at least. I can't promise I won't get insecure again but at least you know how to treat me when I feel like I'm getting third degree burns. Our love can burn as bright as the sun but as long as we are burning together at the same pace and at the same speed I believe that we will be good most definitely. I LOVE YOU TYLER.

Tyler loves me

I love Tyler

he's not going anywhere

I'm not going anywhere.

Tyler loves me (Repeat as many times as needed to feel calm)

A Look At My Love

*You are my destiny. *

Destiny isn't that a concept. A concept where things are laid out and supposed to happen. However I don't think it's that simple. I think we are destined to meet people but we have the will to choose how it happens for instance with love. You can be destined to meet someone just not a certain way. In Greek mythology it is said that Humans originally had two of everything. But Zeus fearing there power split them apart and condemned them to search for one another their entire lives. Which is why I believe when you love someone you become one with one another where you think alike and wear the same clothes every day without thinking.

I think love is To become one. That's what love is, Becoming one with your soulmate but being individuals at the same time.

You are my Everything

You are my lucid drug, one I can't live without. However I don't think you

know that you are the reason that you are the reason I wake up,

the reason that I get out of bed

the reason that I open the curtains in the morning.

A Look At My Love

The feeling you give me is incomparable to the most excitement and love as

anything in this world,

Talking to you through the day makes me feel like a flower that's just blooming

and getting its first taste of sunlight.

This is what it's like to love you so please don't take away my sunlight please

don't let anyone step on me a delicate sunflower that just does one thing blooms

for the sun.

let me continue to bloom for you, until the end of time, until the day I no longer

bloom anymore.

You Consume me

with everything I do I think of you,

I can't help it, I'm in love

I'm completely consumed with you

I know all my love for you to be true

as of when I met you I could tell that it was different

A Look At My Love

*

Hoping you fall as hard as I Do

I don't get it, this Earth has so many people. 7.3 billion people. 7.3 billion

people in the world, it's as full as a cloud in the spring . Which is why I don't

get why I feel so alone, as alone as the first leaf on the ground in fall.

Meaningful connections are hard to come by but I'm just looking for another

leaf to fall with me first so I'm not so alone on the first cold falls day.

Fall with me

And maybe

Just maybe

It won't be so lonely

When I realized it was you and only You

Just as the Earth is drawn to the Sun I am drawn to you!

Gravity keeps pulling me into you keeping me in your orbit making you the

center of my whole universe.

My sun the most important for me to thrive and most importantly be alive but I

undoubtedly have no objections that **you are what I need to pursue.**

A Look At My Love

Even on my Nights out

In a dark smoke filled crowded room

At a bar that I don't even know the name

With my closest friends that adore each other I still feel alone. And I still think

of you. I can feel my subconscious fighting with itself to think about you but

also try to be apart of the conversation. You tend to win my subconscious

thoughts and I think about how your kiss takes me into space and I finally feel

free. I feel free enough to be me. The truth is time stops when I'm with you. A

man made construct simply has no existence. Seconds feel like minutes.

A Look At My Love

minutes feel like hours and this is bliss. Because with you I don't feel so alone.

I know you get me and I get you too.

For when I'm without you

I miss you.

I miss your hair

I miss your laugh

I miss your smile

I can still see it

I can still hear it

And I can still feel it

All the things that make up you I can feel

Just know that I love you

But I am utterly a fool

A Look At My Love

A fool for you

Having Hope in Our Love

What a dark night.

My mind levitates toward you

I can't seem to understand why

And then I look up and I know why

During a full moon my mind tends to wander to you

It's just something about a full moon that

Reminds me how full my life is with you

Reminds me how full my heart is for you

You are my moon and I am your tides

A Look At My Love

I simply didn't exist without you and now that you are gone what am I

I'll tell you

I'm just an empty body of water now

But every time the moon is out my tides come back and suddenly I have

purpose again

Stay this full please.

You are the Only Star I see

Love is a funny thing, it will surround you and consume you as grey clouds can consume a sky! but if you're smart and don't let it consume you the sun will be strong enough to shine through. when the sun does shine through personalities come out and the individualities of one another come out. which is healthy, I also think it's healthy to presume and wonder what he's doing. to wish to be a part of his life as much as a child makes a wish on the brightest star in the sky. 8000 miles can feel like a galaxy away. but I see you in everything that I do. I also tend to believe that's normal. Thinking about you every second of the day has become second nature to me something that I automatically do, just as if it

A Look At My Love

were like breathing. I think that's what love is being an active part of someone's

life.

Fighting For us Every day through Distance

Love isn't always there when you want it. It's not always going to be

convenient, or easy, or practical but when you find it… you have to fight for

it... cause if you don't you risk losing everything.

Blissful Thinking

I can be so happy sometimes, especially when I look at you. you make me the

happiest I've ever felt. Meeting you was like a new galaxy forming, all the stars

and planets coming together and everything is just perfect. I see stars in your

eyes. the way I look at you just says it all, when I'm with you I'm in a trance

A Look At My Love

and to be honest I don't mind being hypnotized. because with you I'm home

and I'm happy.

Falling for you Or with you?

It's not fair you know

When I fall.

When I fall

I fall fast

I fall hard

And when I hit the ground it hurts

Usually

This time it doesn't

You caught me this time

No one else has

I don't think anyone else will

Just don't drop me

A Look At My Love

Because

I know more than most

Gravity hurts

And I can't take it if we reach the ground.

Leaving you Again

I feel alone and scared

The tunnel that is my life is dark and has no lights I can't see

It feels like there is no way out

I wish I could find one

But I'm stuck

For now

But at the end

My light is you.

So this tunnel isn't so bad,

Because my ending is in sight, and it's you.

A Look At My Love

Remembering our kisses While I'm Gone

When I'm with you and I close my eyes it's like I'm blind

Its dark but I see galaxies I see galaxies when I close my eyes and you kiss my lips

gently

I see galaxies when its light and I look into your beautiful eyes

You take me to new places new planets

Maybe I'm not blind at all

Maybe you just help me see.

And you do because when We are together I'm free.

A Look At My Love

Being afraid in my first big boy relationship

I know you are mine

Sometimes I just forget that.

It's almost as if I'm a child and I feel like I own you, I already know I do I already know you are mine. I just get so possessive sometimes. I know you are not my toy. but I'm like a child because I don't understand. I don't know how this works. I'm confused and I'm afraid. I don't want to break you I don't want to break this I don't want to break us.

A Look At My Love

Yearning for you in the Night

When I wake up at night

I scream your name.

I don't yell it

I scream it

because I need you.

my soul is screaming for you and it won't stop

when I'm not with you I'm thinking of you

and when I'm not thinking of you I'm with you.

because I'm always screaming your name and dying of pain, and only your love

can ease my pain.

A Look At My Love

Something we both need to Remember

Timing is a bitch, yes. But it's only a bitch if we let it be. Here's a simple truth that

I think we all need to face up to: *the people we meet at the wrong time are actually*

just the wrong people.

Our timing seems to be spot on.

Let's Grow Together.

My promise to you Is

Tyler,

I'm at a loss for words right now! And you know that is hard for me.

The words I want to say are almost on the tip of my tongue, however I can't

explain it, you leave me speechless and in a state that nobody else has the power to

do. I believe I wrote this out already for you but our love is like a snow globe, it is

fragile it's pretty on the outside but on the inside where nobody can see is a

machine of cogs working and working, people can't see what we are working on

for each other but all they know all we know is that it works and when it works and

when we get our wheels going we make beautiful music. We can have many

symbols to our love which is why I want you to have this ring. It is a replica of

mine and is definitely tied to my heart which belongs to you. So when you feel like

I'm not there or when your lonely look at your ring at think of me and know that

I'm wearing mine too. I haven't taken it off for a year and it would always make

me think of you.

A Look At My Love

You became my home

From the moment I met you I knew you were special

I knew that you would be something important to me

because with you, it is different

with you I feel normal

with you I know who I am

Being with you is like being as comfortable in your home

that was you

you are my home

But homes are a lot of work

And together we can make it work,

White picket fence and all.

A Look At My Love

My new Perspective

Perspective

Eyes aren't they a thing of magic

Light so I can see this magic

But I truly didn't know how to see

I truly didn't know magic

At least that is until I met you.

When you taught me how to identify both.

*

I used to think that in order to be a writer that you had to draw a story or a poem from pain, but the greatest stories of all come from love and the others come from the pain of it. I stopped feeling the pain of love. My writing used to be very one sided. and then I found you. Tyler Biersdorfer. All the pain from my past had went away just as if the sun was shining through clouds that are passing to ruin someone else day.

A Look At My Love

Do you see what you do to me, My entire perspective on life love and most of all writing has changed. My entire mind has shifted and that's because I have found my soulmate.

This is written for him, My soulmate,

All my favorite parts of him, features personality,

Everything

He makes my life easy not hard and I love that.

So Tyler this is exclusively for you, I Love you more than words can express anymore.

BE MY FOREVER <3

Sincerely,

Your Love: Dillon Ryan Longtin

A Look At My Love

A Look At My Love

ISBN 978-1-79488-586-8

9 781794 885868

90000

www.ingramcontent.com/pod-product-compliance
Lightning Source LLC
Chambersburg PA
CBHW081640040426
42449CB00014B/3397